I'm Glad You're Open Weekdays

I'm Glad You're Open Weekdays

Everyday Prayers to the God Who Works between Sundays

BETTY WESTROM SKOLD

AUGSBURG Publishing House • Minneapolis

I'M GLAD YOU'RE OPEN WEEKDAYS
Everyday Prayers to the God Who Works Between Sundays

Copyright © 1985 Augsburg Publishing House

Photos: Bob Combs, 12; Vivienne della Grotta, 17; White Eyes Design, 23; Dale D. Gehman, 31; P. Grant, 48; Jim Cronk, 74; Thomas Judd, 80; Roger W. Neal, 91; Steve Takatsuno, 98; Wallowitch, 101; Rohn Engh, 110.

Library of Congress Cataloging in Publication Data

Skold, Betty Westrom.
    I'M GLAD YOU'RE OPEN WEEKDAYS.

    1. Women—Prayer-books and devotions—English.
I. Title.
BV4844.S56   1985   242'.643   85-3923
ISBN 0-8066-2129-X

Manufactured in the U.S.A.   APH 10-3201

        2   3   4   5   6   7   8   9   0   1   2   3   4   5   6   7   8   9

This book is dedicated
to the memory of my parents, Ted and Marie Westrom,
from whom I caught the notion that God works a seven-day
week, and of my friend, Bonnie Monson,
who lived and died in that same joyous certainty.

Contents

Preface

Books are written to meet a need. The cooking classic *One Thousand and One Interesting Ways to Cook Hamburger* undoubtedly had its beginnings with one person who was made desperate by grocery bills. But there had to be a market. The book could never have made it if there had not been thousands of potential readers who had also been made desperate by grocery bills.

There's a rumor around that you get a best-seller by writing a self-help book. But experience has taught me that self-help is not going to do it. I need more reliable help than me. I need God's help.

And once a week won't do it for me, either. I need God's help seven days a week. Neither my problems nor my "thank yous" can wait for the Sabbath.

On Sundays I revel in the majesty and poetry of public prayer. These prayers, tested by believers through the ages, are as fool-proof as a box cake. But weekdays I just pray from scratch. I'm still awed by the idea of being granted an audience with the King, but somehow the atmosphere is less formal. I rush breathlessly up to the throne of grace in my grubby housework clothes, and I dump out all of my garden variety requests. It's a little like a child pouncing on the Christmas wish book from the mail order house.

Whenever I slow down for a prayer break, I find a God who listens. He may not always grant my requests, but he does not ignore them.

Just as there are thousands of people who look for new ways to cook hamburger, so, too, are there thousands who have prayer conversations with this friendly, weekday God.

When my book *The Kids Are Gone, Lord, But I'm Still Here* was published, my favorite critical endorsement was the spontaneous remark of a reader in New Zealand, who exclaimed, "She knows me!"

That was the idea, of course. I had dared to believe that mothers whose children are grown would find themselves in those pages. I had tried to touch on universal experiences with which the reader could identify.

It pleased me to know that I had reached these "empty nesters," but I also heard rumors that some daughters were reading the book before covering it with Mother's Day gift wrap and that a scattering of husbands were "closet readers."

I'm hoping that all those readers will again sense a bond with me in this new book of reflections and prayer conversations. Because this one is not so specifically aimed at mothers of grown children, perhaps it will speak to an even broader audience.

I am convinced that none of us should be afraid to share our garden variety experiences with our seven-day-a-week God. If we ever get the notion that sparrow-watching is God's main business and that we should be able to handle our own day-to-day problems, we haven't read God's own best-seller very well. In the Bible God asks us to show up often with whatever is on our minds. I, for one, am glad he's open weekdays.

For his good-natured support and interest during the writing of this book I am deeply grateful to the person who shares prayer with me every day of my life, my husband, Bill. Thanks also go to those seven women who took time to "kitchen test" these prayers and to intercept flaws in my manuscript before it went into the hands of the editor. They are Carolyn Carpenter, Lois Johnson, Merle Knutson, Joanne Mau, Jean Miller, Eunice Sheldon, and Carol Uecker.

I'm Glad You're Open Weekdays

Lord, I'm glad you're open weekdays.
It took me a long time to learn that.

Once I tried to keep you
trapped in the church building.

Oh, sure, I looked you up every Sunday,
but I tried to handle
my own troubled Thursday afternoons.

To me, you had always meant candlelight
and organ music
and scrubbed-up prayers.

I had never met the strong carpenter
who hung around
with the down-and-outers.

I had never really listened, Lord.
I had never heard you pleading,
"Don't trap me in your temples.
Let me walk in the market-place,
where the people are.
I am your Savior.
Allow me to function."

I know it now, Lord,
and it makes me glad.
I need every Sunday I can get,
but I'm glad you're open weekdays.

You're Not My Grandfather

You're not my grandfather, Lord.
Why do I talk to you
as if you were?

Gentle? Loving? Kind?
Yes, of course.

But you're not an old softie,
indulging my whims,
protecting me
from my own mistakes,
letting me win at checkers.

You do let me lose, Lord.
You have the good sense
to let me flunk.

And when I butter you up
by saying nice things,
I might as well
hold my breath.
The truth is
I can't pull that on you.
You and I both know
that wheedling isn't prayer.

And where did I get the idea
that you can't hear
as well as you used to?

Why do I set you
in an easy chair
and shout into your good ear?

What makes me think
that your strength is giving out, Lord?

Do I see you as lovable
but a little shaky,
as though you've earned
a gold retirement watch
because of what
you used to be?

You don't wink at my sins, Lord.
You don't look the other way.
I don't have your chuckling approval.
I have your forgiveness.

I love you, Lord,
but you're not my grandfather.
You love me enough to let me fail.

I can talk to you without shouting.
You don't have just one good ear.
You have as many ears
as it takes,
and all of them good.

You really are not my grandfather.
I may grow feeble,
but you are strong forever.

Toward the Sunset

The lid on the mailbox bangs shut,
but I don't rush out to open it.
I can see what the junk mail will be.

There'll be a folder on estate planning,
and one for cemetery plots,
and another about retirement property
in the Ozarks.

Suddenly we're an item
to a different class of advertiser.
We've graduated
to new mailing lists.

Everybody is conspiring
to shove us in the direction
of the sunset.

Maybe I'm hiding out from reality, Lord,
but couldn't this wait for awhile?

I Shoved Ahead of You, Lord

I shoved ahead of you
in the check-out line today, Lord.

And I flared up at you
when you forgot to hang up your coat.

I guess I'd also have to admit
that I snubbed you
at the neighborhood coffee party.

Yesterday was worse.
TV news showed you
sleeping under a bridge
in a cardboard box,
shaving in a public washroom,
standing in line for breakfast
at the mission.

I just yawned,
pushed off the switch,
and went off for a morning
of shopping.

Maybe I'm being
too hard on myself, Lord.
Maybe you didn't mean it
when you taught
that the way we treat others
shows how we feel
about you.

You meant every word,
didn't you, Lord?

When I look into faces around me,
I'm supposed to see you.

The Gift of Words, the Gift of Silence

For the gift of words,
for the gift of silence,
I thank you, Lord.

The uses of words
are quickly learned.
Words are good tools
for wheedling,
for scolding,
for digging out answers.

But it takes awhile
to learn the uses
of silence.

Teachers learn
the value of silence.
Lessons are launched with words,
but the learning takes place
in silence.

If I carry
words into the woods,
I see
only half a forest.

If I raise my voice
I see only a tunnel of trees
and never meet
the creatures that blink
in the darkness.

I only hear
a deer crashing through the brush
or see hoofprints
in damp sand.

But if I go quietly,
that deer might pose
in the clearing.

Silence is my ticket
of admission.

A bird doesn't want applause
for building a nest
or feeding its young.
It just wants
to go about its business.

And I like it that way, Lord.
I want them to treat me
as they treat each other,
with comfortable indifference.

Children need silence, too,
don't they, Lord?

If I strain
to make conversation,
children become wary.
They turn into cardboard figures.

But if I go about
my business silently,
if they half-forget I am there,
I may overhear them
as they really are,
carefree
and honest
and often wise.

In prayer I value
the gift of words,
the gift of silence.

With childlike words
I can tell my need,
but only in silence
can I catch your answer.

Love Everyone? Even the Unlovely?

Agape—
a Greek word,
I guess.
They pronounce it "ah-GAH-pay."

They say it means
to love everyone,
even the unlovely.

They remind me that you did it, Lord.
You paid attention
to all the misfits
that everybody else ignored.
You still do.

And they tell me
It's my job, too, God,
my love assignment.

If people love me,
I love them back.
If someone deserves it,
I can show affection.
But loving the unlovely?
How could I do that?

Well, today I watered my houseplants,
those miserable misfits
by my kitchen window.

They're limp.
They're straggly.
They have done nothing
to deserve my devotion.

They haven't even had
the good sense
to die.

But against all logic
I hang in there.
I feed them.
I water them.
I even talk to them
when nobody else is around.

The truth is
I'm committed.

Agape?
Well, maybe.

Two Ways of Gardening

We're back from our evening walk, Lord,
and we noticed
at the house on the corner
they're using a sturdy ground cover,
and a block away
they've decided on crushed rock.

Backyard engineers are solving
"the problem."
Landscaping has become a defensive action.
Flower growing has given way
to weed prevention.

Our neighbors are all doing battle
with crabgrass
and chickweed
and volunteer maple seedlings.

Nothing can sprout
through the armor of black plastic,
the carpet of wood chips.

In place of the smiling gardener
who scooped up an armful of daisies
or showed off his prize tomatoes
we have only the cold technician
with his "fortress gardening."

They're two different things, aren't they,
vanquishing weeds
and coaxing flowers to grow?

There are two ways of gardening, Lord,
and two ways of reading your book.

We can focus on the Law,
fiercely holding back the weeds of evil,

or we can look to the joyous colors
of the gospel.

Weedlessness is a grim substitute
for the bright bloom of forgiveness
and new life.

Does Your Church Disappoint You?

The church was your idea, Lord.
The truth, now,
doesn't it disappoint you?

You must have noticed the sham,
the collection of vices
that we choose to call
"human frailty."

The characters in the pew—
the stout man in the polyester suit,
and the girl with the smeary mascara
and the faded lady with the tired eyes—
they seem miscast (wouldn't you say?).
They seem too ordinary to carry out
your extraordinary dream.

Isn't your glorious vision
sagging into dullness?

There's no passion, Lord,
unless you count
those who bristle with indignation
at the hymnal editor
who left out the fourth verse
of a favorite song.

There are no heroes.
Only the shallow reformer
who wants to save the soul
of the church
by tinkering around
with the worship forms.

You may hear
scattered voices declaring
"The church must change,"
but don't get your hopes up, Lord.

What they're saying is,
"We've got to give it more class."

You mean
you knew this would happen, Lord?
It doesn't surprise you?

You mean
you're not dismayed
by the squabbling
and the pride
and the coldness?

When you dreamed about your church,
did you know
that one day people would yawn
at the plight of the unsaved?

I guess you take the long view.
You see problems,
but you remember the church
in its moments of greatness.

You have seen it honeycombed with evil,
then swept clean
by winds of reform.

You are able to see what I can't.
Even now
there may be some quiet heroism
in the lives of this ordinary
cast of characters.

Help me to see it, God.
Help me to believe with you
that the remarkable life
of the church
is more than the combined total
of our unremarkable lives.

Easy Chair Equality

I'm not an official,
card-carrying feminist, Lord,
but if I were,
I'd paint me a banner
(orange letters, I think),
a banner reading
"Equality in the Easy Chair."

Where is it written that a man
has a divine right
to the most comfortable chair
in the house?

Next Father's Day, we're advised,
give old dad
a big, squashy, softly-upholstered,
outpost of heaven.
Let him lean back serenely
with his feet propped
on a retractable footrest.

That leaves mother sitting primly
on a stiff, little, second-best job
that neither reclines nor squashes
nor supports the feet.

Sometimes I cheat, Lord.
Sometimes, when he isn't around,
I sneak a sit on that leather recliner;
but I've been conditioned
to connect easy chairs and fathers,
and before long the guilt feelings set in.

I get to my feet
and move to the misery
of "my chair."

I'm wondering, Lord,
does that mean
I'm not liberated?

Forgiving Takes Awhile

The basic act of forgiveness
is no problem.

Traditional phrases come easily:
"I understand."
"That's OK."
"Let's forget it."

But after the words of forgiveness
there is still that awkward time
of beginning again,
of trying to feel at ease
with that person.

Like a child holding up
two pieces of a broken cookie,
I ask the impossible,
"Lord, fix it.
Make it whole again."

For nations
peace doesn't happen
the moment signatures are scribbled
on a pact.

After guns grow silent,
it is not enough to clear away wreckage,
to bandage wounds.

Nations must learn
to breathe easily,
to go about their business.

It is necessary
to build something,
some sort of a bridge.

I really have put aside
this hurt, Lord.
My anger has cooled,
but there is something stubborn
inside me
that doesn't trust the truce.

I must move
from that first shaky smile
to serenity of spirit.

Each of us is putting
the other on trial.
We're still testing, Lord.

Help us both to believe
that our new bridge
will carry the weight.

A Crazy Kind of Therapy

I cleaned stove burners today, Lord,
and it felt good.
Strangely enough,
I enjoyed it.

What's great about rubbing greasy specks
with a scratchy pad?

What's good about gritty cleanser
and ammonia smell
and a pile of blackened paper towels
in the wastebasket?

What's interesting about
two curls of uncooked macaroni
in the reflector pan?

Maybe it's a crazy kind of therapy.
You see, I have a whole list of things
I can do nothing about.
I can't make myself over
into a saint or a dazzling beauty,
I can't decide things for other people.
I can't bring perfection to the world.

But if I narrow the focus
to four encrusted stove burners,
there is something I can do.

I can't make them new again,
but I can do something,
something that shows.

They Believed—Help Thou Their Unbelief

Lord, when I pray
for unbelievers
who haven't found you yet,
I am not discouraged.

Many of them will come looking for you.
They will come humbly, with hope.

But what can I say
for those who used to believe,
for those who once held on to your hand
and have chosen to let go?

What do I say to the wounded,
casualties of the daily struggle,
the bruised ones who fling their challenge,
"The God I knew
wouldn't have let this happen"?

How do I reach the friend
who has sinned and loathes himself,
who feels too soiled
to walk in your company?

What do I say to the woman
whose possessions possess her,
who has grown rich
and has paid too high a price?

What can I do
for the person who loved you
and doesn't anymore,
for the follower
who has wandered off on his own,
for the tested one
who got stuck
on your multiple choice questions?

I have to really want them back,
don't I, Lord?
And I can't be afraid to say so.

But why do I act
as though it all depends on me,
as though I can worry them back to you.

I must stand back
and let your Spirit go to work.

I have to remember,
You want them back, too.

"Go into Your Closet and Pray"

There's one verse in the Bible
that bothers me, Lord.
It's that verse that says
"Go into your closet and pray."

The closet?
And pray?
It's a jungle in there.

Maybe some people
are just born closet cleaners.
I'm not.

Still, if I could manage it,
If I could squeeze myself in
and pray with my eyes open,
I might learn something,
Maybe even repentance.

For one thing,
I lay up for myself treasures.
I buy more than I need.
My clothes aren't just for warmth
or for modesty.

They're for pleasing myself
or for showing off.

I seem to lay up for myself
nontreasures, too.
Once something is mine,
it is mine forever.
I hate good-byes,
even to miniskirts
and worn-out sandals.

Dust kittens in the corners
reproach me.
Do I concentrate
on just the cleaning that shows?

Another day I'll bring you
my big problems, Lord,
and, if you don't mind,
I'll face those out in the open.

But the closet has taught me
something about secret sins,
something about piling up treasures.

The closet has reminded me,
"There's a time to keep
and a time to cast away."

Why Can't We Talk?

Why can't we talk, Lord?
Why can't we hear each other?

Parent and child,
husband and wife,
pastor and people.

We don't listen,
can't seem to hear.

White and black
are deaf to each other.
The wealthy tune out on the poor.

All strangers—
nobody listening
to anybody else.

Babel keeps happening, Lord.
Pride has built still another tower.
In our drive to be our own gods
we build towers,
and lose each other
in the process.

God, help us to pull down the towers.
We don't like being strangers.
We need to talk, Lord.
Send us Pentecost.

Lord, You Are Light

The Light of the world, yes,
but, Lord, you are my light, too.

You are candlelight,
bathing this room with beauty.
You are sunlight,
strengthening sunlight.

You are my trouble light
when something needs repair,
my night light,
comforting your child,
my searchlight,
sweeping across darkness.

And one day, Lord,
you will be my porch light,
welcoming me home.

Lord, Help My Friend

We talked on the phone for an hour, Lord,
because she needed it
and because she knew
I'd listen.

She dumped out her load
of guilt and remorse
and sadness.

She needed help, Lord,
and I wanted to give it,
but it was like trying to bake a pie
in a motel room.
I simply wasn't equipped.

Despair has become her best friend,
and I couldn't really help her.

I couldn't help her, Lord,
but you could.
I promised you would.
Is that OK?

I passed along some things you've said,
words of hope and forgiveness.

I invited her to look you up.
I said I was sure you'd care.

She's scared, Lord.
She's bitter and lost
and confused.

If you haven't heard from her,
you will soon.

Thank you for your answer.

May She Find Home

She's grown frail, Lord.
Her hands tremble,
and she nods off while we're visiting.

This loved person has grown old,
and today she's a little scared.

Today she
and a handful of her things
are being transplanted
into the nursing home.

There's been a sorting process,
things being packed into boxes.

Memories, too, are being sorted.
Her health and power are diminished now,
but we treasure memories of her strength.
That strength has left a mark
on all our lives.

We owe her more than memories.
Memories can wear thin from handling.

She hugs the past,
but she has more
than the past.
She has us to hug.

In our family
there are no "has beens," Lord.
Help her to know she can count on us.
Help us to make every visit
a fresh expression of our concern.

Be with her in this new setting, Lord.
May she find tenderness
and comfort
and a sense of home.

What Have They Done?

What have they done?
The thought clings
like a wood tick.

Doesn't anyone care anymore?
What have they done
to the woods where we used to camp
and to the sleepy town
where we bought our groceries?

I remember these woods
as they once were,
sunlight slicing
through tall trees,
the road, a narrow hallway,
with walls of
ragged-topped red pine.

But what have they done?
Now motorcycles roar along the trails,
and in the town
strings of plastic pennants
flutter above the car lot.

In the enclosure
lazy deer
pace sawdust-covered ground,
begging corn
from the tourists.

I am outraged.
"What greedy stranger
has strode through the forest,
cheapening it
with his clutter?"

A stranger?
Probably not.
It may not be
that city stranger, at all,
who has scattered ugliness.

That could be his vacation place,
half-hidden from the road,
in tune with the forest.

Who is to blame
for the ugliness?
It could be some kid
who grew up in these woods
who painted his house bright blue
and planted a whirling, plastic sunflower
beside it.

Maybe, because the forest
had always been there,
he didn't see it at all,
never knew
that it was beautiful.

It does happen,
doesn't it, Lord?
We take things for granted,
and something beautiful is lost.

Is it callous strangers
who have cheapened your gospel?
Probably not.

I grew up with your story.
I'm used to it.
For me, it has always been around.

Do I even notice
the wonder of it?

The thought clings
like a wood tick.

For New Beginnings

Thank you, God,
for new beginnings,
for the crazy, stubborn hope
that whispers,
"Go ahead.
Pick yourself up.
Start over."

A slumbering volcano erupts,
and we are grabbed by fear.

The rivers of hot mud,
the death cloak of gray ash,
trees ripped away and flattened,
the mountain still muttering
death threats.

But nature heals its own wounds.
After forest fire,
after floods,
after blaze of battle,
wounded places shrug off death,
refuse to take it too seriously.

One at a time at first,
then by the hundreds,
the things of nature choose life.

A flower pokes up
through gray ash.

Feathery beginnings
of grass
touch the slope with green.

A new generation
of tree seedlings
stakes out a claim
to the forest.

When I am wounded, Lord,
when I try to pray
but come up empty,
when I get the feeling
that every joy has been ripped away
and flattened,
coated with ashes,
send me hope.

Wounds do heal, Lord.
In everything you have created,
wounds heal.

Tell me to shrug off despair,
to choose life,
to start over.

The Parable of the Blue Jeans

I like your parables, Lord.
Plain talk,
but they make good reading.

The mustard seed,
the lost sheep,
the farmer's barn—
all teach me something.

Now it's fun
to spot my own parables,
those familiar, weekday symbols
of some deeper meaning.

You've plopped me down
in the middle
of a whole world
of do-it-yourself parables.

I just have to keep my eyes open
and learn to read them.

For example, blue jeans.
Aren't they today's resurrection symbol,
our everyday reminder
that some things are indestructible?

The kids know that jeans
may be temporarily out of commission,
but they are never too tattered
for rebirth.

For as long as patches
are available,
there is hope.
They can be restored
to faded usefulness.

And, when all else fails,
for the true believer,
blue jeans can be reborn,
born again as cutoffs.

Were You Yawning?

Did you feel
like yawning, too, God?
I thought tonight's meeting
would never end.
There was no spark to it.

We plodded through
our usual routine,
combing the minutes for misspellings,
solemnly using
this year's favorite words:
"prioritize"
and "feedback"
and "cash flow."

We don't wrestle
with problems, Lord.
We fuss about them.
We have become
list-makers.

If there was
a prophetic voice in the crowd,
it had developed
laryngitis.

Half listening,
my mind called the roll
of your heroes:

Moses parting the Red Sea,
David facing the giant,
Luther defiantly nailing
his challenge
to the church door,
Joan of Arc facing death
for her "voices."

And the disciples, of course,
that little band of castoffs
who became "new men."

I kept wishing
they'd all stop by
before adjournment.

But you know, Lord,
the scary part is
that at our church
John the Baptist
and St. Paul
and Martin Luther
would never get elected.

For the Joy of Singing

Thank you
for the joy of singing, Lord,
for the way it feels
to take a deep breath
and just let the song come out.

I guess the expression
"joyful noise"
was invented for me.
I just want to sing
hymns in praise of things . . .
all sorts of things.

In church I pour my share
into a great sea of sound
and I am not offended
if other voices drown me out.

I challenge them.
We drown each other out.

When I sing
I am not trying to catch
anyone's ear, Lord.
I know I have your ear,
and it accepts my song
and maybe even hears it
as something beautiful.

When the concert singer performs,
I listen
and I enjoy it.
But there's something better.
Doing it is better.

My kids never understood
about that, Lord.
They were always embarrassed
if I sang out.

They would sigh
and raise their eyes
toward the ceiling.

The message was clear.
"I know you mean it, Mom,
but could you keep it down?"

And, now that I think about it,
my dad used to sing
right out in church.

And I remember looking toward the ceiling
and wishing he'd keep it down.

And you know, Lord,
(it must be hereditary)
it didn't change a thing.

"—But Not Politics or Religion"

Am I wrong, Lord?
Is it indelicate
to talk about
politics and religion?

There is an approved list, you know,
safe topics for conversation,
a seal of approval attached.

Fashions? OK.
Football? Why not?
Recipes?
Fad diets?
Both harmless topics.
Only what happens to our world
is off limits.

Just two topics
are taboo,
politics and religion.

"Divisive," they warn,
so we engage
in superficial chatter
or we are shushed
into polite silence.

But isn't it better,
divided by something real
than uniting around a soap bubble?

The despot
and the false prophet
stride across the land
unchallenged,
while liberties are trampled
and voiceless disciples
keep their love a secret.

I am not convinced, God.
I think of Peter,
how it must have been for him,
after Calvary.

Peter had a long time to remember
that other night,
shivering by the fire,
feeling the emptiness.

Peter had a long time
to wish he had dared
to talk about politics
and religion.

Forgiveness Means Reunion

They spoke of your forgiveness, Father,
but joylessly,
using prison terminology.

I pictured
a released convict
walking out through stone gates,
freed on some legal technicality.

I could see the prisoner,
uncomfortable in his new clothes,
looking over his shoulder,
afraid of being called back.

It's not that way, Lord.
Your forgiveness is better than that.
There's more joy in it.

When you forgive me,
I'm not outside a prison gate.
I'm walking through the gate
of an airport,
back from wherever I've been.

Forgiveness is you and I
running to meet each other.
It is love.
It is joy.
It is reunion.

"The Real World"

They call it "the real world," Father,
and they make it sound logical,
but I'd like a second opinion.

"The real world,"
they seem to be saying,
"is no place
for you starry-eyed believers,
no place for hope
and joy
and naive forgiveness.

Don't come around
with your smiley, Sunday school answers.

That isn't the way
the real world works.

The real world is built
for grabbing and gouging
and getting even."

And I see kids
in sweaty practice jerseys
being taught to commit fouls
as basic strategy.

"In the real world ...
the real world ...
the real world. ..."

We hear the message:
"Adjust.
Make yourself comfortable
in the presence of evil."

What were you thinking, Father,
on that seventh day,
when you looked down
at what your hands had made,
shimmering in new light?

Didn't you look down
at your world
(smiling, maybe)
and didn't you call it "real"?

I've Been Forgetting Things

I've been forgetting things lately, God,
dumb little memory slips
like cooking coffee without grounds in the basket
or forgetting the stamp on the envelope
or losing track of which day the committee meets.

But thank you, Lord,
that my memory still works
for the things that count.

I still remember pine smells and loon calls
at Lake Itasca.
I remember the first chocolate cake
that Billy made from scratch,
and Tom's first reaction to fireworks
"like crumbs from God."

I remember coming home late
to find a trail of paper clues,
the treasure hunt the kids had laid out
to surprise us.

I haven't forgotten my mother's washday soup
or my dad's male quartet
or Bill's quiet nod of approval
for my wedding gown.

Thank you, God,
for the remembering that counts.

I'm No Bargain

I've been cost-conscious, Lord.
I've had to be.
I've studied price tags.

I've had to design budgets
around threadbare snowsuits
and broken glasses,
transmission repairs, orthodontia,
and tuition payments.

I've pored over thick Sunday papers,
noted the clearance ads,
then, like a gladiator,
steeled myself to do battle
for whatever the fashionable shoppers
had left behind.

It's become habit, Lord,
focusing on the price tag,
always the price tag.

You have loved me, Lord,
accepted me,
sins and all.

You have loved me,
and for you, the price was
—and still is—
unbelievably high.

But for once
I don't grab for the price tag

Why don't I study it
with my usual intensity?

Maybe I'd rather not be reminded, Lord,
Maybe I'd rather step around the question,
"Am I worth it?"

Accepting the Risk

It looks out of place
in the parking lot, Lord,
the handsome car
parked at a strange angle—
"kitty-corner," we used to call it.

That angle says,
"I'm special.
Don't scratch me.
Lined up parallel
with ordinary cars,
I could be scarred."

My life is parked close
to other lives, Lord,
and that makes me vulnerable.

If I line up according to the pattern,
if I involve myself,
I risk something.

I must protect myself.
I'm special.

Often, maybe too often,
I park "kitty-corner," Lord,
warning other lives
to keep their distance.

You did park close, Lord,
and for you it meant scars.

Only if I allow myself to park close
to other lives,
only if I risk being scarred,
only then is my life
lined up with yours.

We Need to Plan

I don't mean to keep
bringing this up, Lord,
but how far
will our money have to stretch?

If we just knew
how long we have left
(I mean roughly)
we could make long-range plans.

If we knew,
we wouldn't have to hold back
on helping the children
or sharing with the needy.

Has a date been set?
Have you made plans
for cuing in that final trumpet?

I know we're supposed to trust, Lord,
but could you give us
a ball-park figure?

Yes, I remember,
lilies of the field
and sparrows
and all that.

But of course that was before inflation.
Do you mean...
could you really mean...
not worry
at all?

How Did You Dare?

How did you dare
to tell your story
before the world was ready, Lord?

Wouldn't it have been better
to wait
until the technology was in place?

How did you dare
to set your story down
in the mind of a herdsman
and a fisherman
and a tentmaker?

How could you trust
your message
to the uncertainties
of a village grapevine?

Didn't you worry
that it would get lost . . .
or garbled?

It's better now, of course . . .
printing presses,
television,
copying machines.

There's not much danger
of losing track of the message.

What are you saying, Lord?
Witnessing?
You mean one-on-one?
Well, there is a committee, I guess.
I was on it once,
for a year or two.

You mean every one of us, Lord?
The grapevine thing again?
You still want your story to spread
by word of mouth?

My On-the-Job Training

There were books for mothers, Lord,
but they left things out.

The books talked about creativity,
but they never told me it was messy.
They never mentioned paint spatters
and glue spills
and sawdust piles.

Books never warned me
that tools wander off
or that Scotch tape and ballpoint pens
must be cleverly hidden.

The books said
kids should express themselves.
They never explained how to fit
a green and orange Mother's Day project
into a subtle color scheme.

Books never taught me
what constitutes a treasure,
or how guilty I'd feel
about throwing a broken toy
or a speckled stone
or some other treasure
into the trash.

The books never mentioned
that life-and-death issues
can be handled more easily
than daily repeatables
like tipping milk glasses.

Books taught me to bake
a picture-book cake,
but nobody mentioned
that kids prefer Hostess Twinkies.

The books gave me
fine prayers to recite,
but I never knew
I'd get so tired
that bedtime would feel
like a benediction.

I had read that sometimes
kids want to run away from home,
but I learned for myself
that sometimes mothers do, too.
The books told me
that babies get their days and nights mixed up,
but nobody ever told me
that teenagers do, too.

According to books,
a child's first day of school
is an adjustment for mom, but nobody told me
how tough the last day would be.

I've never been Mother-of-the-Year, Lord,
but thank you for every year
I've been mother.
Thank you for every lesson
I've been able to learn
the hard way.

Thank you for the most exasperating,
baffling,
terrifying,
intriguing,
on-the-job training
that's ever been devised.

Seedtime

I push damp, crumbly dirt
over the seeds in the furrow
and press it down with the heel
of my hand,
then I get stiffly to my feet,
brush myself off,
and wash over the row
with a gentle spray from the hose.

Our hopes are high, Lord.
They always are, at planting time.

We dream of a bumper crop
of radishes and string beans
and zinnias.
We'd better dream that way
or we have no business
scattering seed.

But things can happen
on the way to a bumper harvest—
cutworms,
scalding winds,
killing frost.
Our enthusiasm may cool.
Weeds might take over.

What is there about gardening?
It was mankind's first assignment,
of course.
Maybe it's the best way of learning
that we're dependent on you.

Adam and Eve
never got that straight.
They forgot who was in charge
of the Garden.

I don't want to make the same mistake
on the way to the harvest.

Send rain and sunshine, Lord.
Bless this good seed,
and keep reminding me
who is in charge of the garden.

Drown Proofing

From the shoreline
I watch them
bobbing in the water,
children in a beginner's class
learning drown proofing.

It could come in handy,
they're told.
It's a way of resting.
Not a stroke for making headway,
but a method
for keeping afloat.
There's a minimum of effort involved
so you don't wear yourself out.

Am I doing the same thing
with my life, Lord,
just bobbing around,
keeping my head above water?

Have I settled
for a minimum effort?
Have I given up on the idea
of getting somewhere?

Teach me a strong stroke, Lord.
Drown proofing isn't good enough.

Do They See Me?

Do my children see me, God?
No, not just as mother.
As person.
Do they really see me?

It took me awhile,
a long while,
before I really saw
my own mother.

When I was young
and my step was light,
I saw her,
plump, middle-aged,
her apron dusted with flour.

I saw her
sorting laundry,
frowning at grocery slips
and report cards,

and you know, Lord,
I never really believed
those old photographs.

I never believed
the slim young girl
in leg o'mutton sleeves,
leaning against a Model T,
smiling up at boyfriends.

I didn't believe
the laughing girl in the crazy hat,
showing off for the camera.

I didn't believe
the soft-eyed bride,
looking demurely
down at her bouquet.

Then I was plump and middle-aged.
Flour dusted my apron.
I was sorting laundry.
I was frowning
at grocery slips and report cards.

She had grown old.
Her hair was white
and she walked unsteadily
with her cane.

We talked for awhile, Lord.
I don't even remember
what was said,
but suddenly it happened.

Suddenly I believed
those old photographs.

Even a Small Parade

Thank you for kindliness, Lord,
for everyday signs
of gentleness and decency
wherever we run across them.

Thank you for today,
and that family of ducks
waddling in a poky processional
across the highway.

Traffic stopped.
Hands relaxed on steering wheels.
A smile passed
from one front seat to another.

Five drivers,
motors idling,
willing to take note
of even a small parade.

Five drivers,
caught in the act of being human,
and enjoying it.

Saturday Was for Getting Ready

Sunday was taken seriously
in my childhood,
and Saturday night was a time
for getting ready.

Saturday meant
a shampoo
with vinegar rinse,
a bath in the tin tub,

memorizing the catechism
from a thin red book
or a thin blue one.

And it was on Saturday night
that my father gathered up the shoes
and performed his weekly ritual.

Working on the enamel-topped table
in the warmth of the kitchen range,
he daubed paste wax
on everyday brown oxfords
and buffed them
to a Sunday shine.

Then he lined them up
in a neat row,
confident that his five kids
would meet the Sunday standard.

Now, Lord,
in a world where Sunday
is approached more casually,
where worship is squeezed in between
a snowmobile ride
and a shopping spree,
I remember those other Sundays.

I remember marching down the aisle
with offering pennies tied into the corner
of my handkerchief.
I remember dad directing the choir
and mother shaking hands
with the farmers' wives.

And, Lord, sometimes I think I sensed
that my shiny brown oxfords
were standing on holy ground.

My Diet Isn't Working

I'm not doing well
on my diet, Lord.

Like Joseph,
I have seen both the fat years
and the lean years,
but just now
famine is not my problem.

Just now the arrow
on the scale swings upward,
and the doctor frowns.
Now the saleswoman directs me
to the size 16s.

Did Ecclesiastes mention
a time for eating
and a time to refrain from eating?

Well, my spirit is willing, Lord,
but my flesh reaches out
for pork chops and pizza
and cherry pie.

I've renounced them all,
and I meant it.
But it's taken me three weeks
to lose two-thirds of a pound.

Lord, grant me strength of character
and an appetite for celery sticks.

The Far Country

In some ways, Lord,
getting them through the teen years
was like being the father
of the prodigal son.

I think of all those nights
when I lay sleepless in my bed,
waiting to hear the rolling
of the garage door.

Each time,
for each of the children,
that garage door sound
meant that they had come back
from some far country.

For the father of the prodigal,
the far country meant a distant place
of spectacular wickedness.

For me, on those nights,
the far country was any place
beyond our lot line,
where unknown dangers
lay in wait.

For me, the far country
was any place
away from my motherly eye,
where I couldn't tag along.

The prodigal's father and I
had much in common,

but at least
when he prepared a feast
and killed a fatted calf,
nobody phoned to say,
"By the way,
I won't be home for dinner."

Teach Me to Listen—to Myself

Lord, teach me to listen . . .
to myself.

Make me turn a critical ear
to the words that I dump out
lavishly on others.

Remind me to measure out
in smaller helpings
my wit and my wisdom.

Force me to hear
my tedious repetitions.

Show me the limits
of my expertise.

And, Lord, when others are talking,
grant me the humility
to wait my turn.

You Might Not Fit In

I'm not sure you'd fit in
anymore, Lord.
We've learned a new way
of looking at things.
"Me psychology"
has come into fashion.

It's now "demeaning"
to sweep a street
or clean a building
or make a pot of coffee.

I'm not sure what we'd think
about washing each other's feet
or offering to sit
at the wrong end of the table.

If you came around
with that "servanthood" approach again,
I'm not sure we'd listen.

Officially we do display concern
for outcasts, Lord,
It's even somewhat fashionable
to worry about criminals
and prostitutes.

We just handle it
a little differently.

We work through a committee
or a support group.
We write to our congressman
about social change.

It's not quite the same thing
as asking them to dinner,
but it's not as if
we didn't care.

Frankly, Lord, I'm not sure
you'd fit in anymore,
but then I guess
you never did.

Making Disciples Is No Snap

"Go ye, therefore
and make disciples."
I heard your words, Lord,
and they sounded
like a fanfare,
a drumroll.
I was stirred into action.

But when I rang the doorbell
the excitement drained away.

Making disciples is no snap, Lord.
Pleasant people answer the bell.
They smile, but they don't hear
the drumroll.

To them,
you have less practical importance
than their analyst
or their golf pro
or their hairdresser.

The good news
is no news to them.
They've read the story,
or at least the headlines,
then they've set it aside
for the next paper drive.

Making disciples is no snap, Lord,
but, how about it,
should I try again?

Limits to Our Kindliness

Kindliness is a way of life
in the suburbs, Lord,
the bird feeders on our patios
advertise that.

Of course we have to be
a little careful.
We choose seed that will draw
only the right class of birds
to our feeders.

Blue jays are too pushy,
and the common grackle
is a little too common,
and if we cater to the sparrows
it could get out of hand.

It's worth a little extra money
to buy feed
that suits the cardinals
and the chickadees.
They're an ornament
to anyone's backyard.

And don't we shop
for ingenious devices
to make squirrels feel unwelcome?

We like to show kindliness
to people, too, Lord,
but again there are problems.

Of course we want to be decent
to everyone,
but it's hard to invite just anyone
to be our dinner guests.

People come in assorted colors.
They come with pleasant faces
or sneering ones.
They come with negative attitudes
and weird life-styles
and irritating habits.

Do you mean we should invite them all, Lord?
Are you serious?
I know you had dinner with sinners
and tax collectors,
but is all that necessary?

Is it so bad
to be a little selective?

Reservation Confirmed

When you made
your historic visit, Lord,
you never visited our town.
Our town
wasn't even on the map.

Now the visitor has gone,
but you are here—
in my town
at my house.

The visitor has gone,
but you've moved in to stay.
You're here,
helping me to deal
with my loneliness
and my terror.

You're here,
brushing over
the gray of my sorrow
with the bright colors
of hope.

Our town isn't impressive, Lord,
but you and I are in it together. And meanwhile
I believe your promise.

Meanwhile it's good to know
I have a confirmed reservation
in a better place.

I'm a Collectible

I have friends who know about these things.
They tell me there's a difference
between a genuine antique
and a "collectible."

And I think I've got it figured out, Lord.
I've become a "collectible."

I'm at that awkward age . . .
not quite old enough
to be treated with reverence
like a treasured antique,

but old enough
to be a "collectible" . . .
a little out-of-date,
somewhat amusing,
not worth a lot,
not to be taken too seriously.

Some day I may become a genuine antique . . .
revered for my wisdom,
valued for my judgment,
mellowed into a priceless treasure.

Some day I may be taken seriously,
but frankly, Lord,
I can wait.

I Was the Only One Around

She was calling for help, Lord.
The tears
wouldn't stop coming.
She spilled out her fears
at my kitchen table.

And I couldn't send
technical assistance
or form a committee.

There was no way
to arrange for
a feasibility study.

I was the only one around
to help her ...
(or you and I
were the only ones around).

But how could I help her?
To be honest, Lord,
I had no strength to share,
no bandage of wisdom
for her wounds.

Then you spoke to me, Lord.
(I'm sure it was you.)

"You don't have to be perfect,"
you told me.
"Share your weakness.
Share your doubts.
Then she can look
at her own weakness
without shame."

So I did it, Lord.
We talked and we prayed
and I let my weakness show.

And (you were right)
it seemed
to bring her strength.

At least for that day
it seemed
to bring her strength.

How Did It Feel?

How did it feel, Lord,
creating the heavens
and the earth?

Did you smile
as you hung the universe in place
like an awesome mobile?

Did you laugh out loud,
designing the giraffe?

And, like a mother
dropping jelly beans
into piles,
("one for you,
one for you,
and one for you"),
did you deliberately
dole out beauty
with an impartial hand?

In that place
a pile of mountains,
and over there
a scattering of lakes,
like bright beads
from a broken necklace,
then
somewhere else
forests marching down
to the sea?

And did you tremble
when you fashioned us,
yearning,
imperfect,
free?

We don't understand
all of it, God.

We ask ourselves questions.

We can't agree
about why you did it
or how you did it.

We puzzle
over your timetable.

But we do agree on one thing.
You created it with love, Lord.
It shows.

They'll Both Learn to Talk

I stand at the nursery window, Lord,
and she stands beside me
in her quilted robe,
peering through the glass.

And I know
without comparing plastic bracelets
which of the pinkish babies
belongs to her.

It is that one
in the crib nearest the window,
the yawning boy
with the fuzzy cap of brown hair.
She focuses on him.

She winces if the child cries.
She smiles as he blinks.
She talks softly and taps on the glass,
then waves good-bye
before walking back down
the scrubbed corridor.

The young mother is ready, Lord.
She's learned about bathing
and diapering
and nursing the baby.

And, when the time comes,
she's ready to teach,
single words at first,
like "daddy" and "puppy."

Later he'll string words together,
"I'm sorry,"
or "I love you,"
or "I'll come right home
after school."

Should I have told her, Lord?
Shall I tell her now
that she'll have to learn to talk, too?
There are mother words
she'll need to know.

"Did you remember your notebook?"
and "Don't come in with your boots on."
"Would you eat those crackers
over the sink?" and
"It'll hurt for just a minute."

She'll learn to say,
"If I've told you once
I've told you a hundred times"
and "You should have thought about that
before you bought it."

And finally,
sooner than she knows,
she'll learn to say,
"Yes, I'll accept the charges."

I Had Her Labeled

Judging her
was quick work, Lord.
The signs were all there.

With one glance,
I measured her worth,
attached a label,
and filed her under "S."
"S" for "superficial."
"S" for "silly."

She seemed interested
only in the length
of her fingernails.

Her only talent
was staying thin.

And that smile!
Every morning
she just set it on "automatic"
and let it run
all day.

"Silly,
superficial."
The label fit.

But then I heard things, Lord,
rumors that made me uneasy.

I heard scraps of talk
that forced me to look again.

Her mother had spent
three years in dying, they said,
and she was the one
who had learned to give bed baths
and to struggle with mountains
of messy laundry.

She was the one
who had set every dinner tray
with white linen
and garden flowers.

I heard how she spearheaded
a neighborhood crime watch
and how she's been helping out
at the shelter for battered women.

It's hard to admit it,
but I had misjudged her, Lord.
Thank you for changing my mind.

Lord, Teach Me to Pray

Edit my prayers, Lord.
I used to think
I had a way with words,
but now I'm asking you,
would you edit my prayers?

When my words
slide out too easily,
when I pay more attention
to style than to substance,
when I get carried away
by my own "way with words,"

Lord, teach me to pray
(I mean really pray).

Weed out the excess
with a firm pencil.

Help me to pray lean prayers—
basic, honest, stripped down
to a scream for help,
a shout of joy,
a cry of shame.

Then, Lord, teach me to grab
on to your hand
in one long moment
of wordless prayer.